THE NEW PLANT LIBRARY

HOSTAS

THE NEW PLANT LIBRARY

HOSTAS

ANDREW MIKOLAJSKI

Consultant: Diana Grenfell
Photography by Peter Anderson

AURA

This edition published in 1997 by
Aura Books plc
14-15 Fairway Drive
Greenford
Middlesex UB6 8PW

Produced by Anness Publishing Limited
Hermes House
88-89 Blackfriars Road
London SE1 8HA

ISBN 0 947793 33 X

Publisher Joanna Lorenz
Senior Editor Clare Nicholson
Designer Michael Morey

Printed in Hong Kong

3 5 7 9 10 8 6 4 2

Contents

Introduction

Foliage plants *par excellence*, hostas are indispensable in the garden. The largest are some of the stateliest of hardy perennials and are universally rated as among the stars of the summer border, but there are also a number of dwarfs that frolic in shady rock gardens or in peat beds. Most can be grown successfully in containers so they make ideal patio plants. This book, with its portraits of some of the most notable hostas grown today, gives some idea of the huge range available and shows you how to care for these rewarding plants.

■ RIGHT
A sumptuous planting of 'Snowden' with the stately *Hydrangea aspera* subspecies *aspera*, both at their peak in late summer.

The history of hostas

Hostas originate in the Far East, with most species occurring in the damp woodland areas of Japan, some in conjunction with ferns and grasses. Many are found in more open areas of high rainfall. Most grow in rich, deep, fertile soil, but a few species, particularly the smaller ones, grow in the moss on tree trunks or rocks.

Hostas first reached the West in the 1790s but the name *Hosta*, honouring the Austrian botanist Nicholas Thomas Host, was not proposed until 1812, before which they had been included within *Hemerocallis* (the daylilies). The name *Funkia* was also sometimes used, and this has lingered on as a common name. The first hostas to arrive in Europe were *H. plantaginea* and *H. ventricosa,* both Chinese species; they are still highly rated garden plants. Plant hunting continues and some new species are still being discovered in Japan, Korea and elsewhere in the Far East.

Hostas were included in the family Liliaceae which includes lilies and daylilies along with many other genera, but they are now often placed in their own family, Hostaceae. Modern thinking divides the genus into about 40 species and well over 1000 cultivars. However, these

■ OPPOSITE
In this fascinating scheme a blue-leaved hosta offsets the ripening pink seeds of *Paeonia mlokosewetischii. Clematis* 'Huldine' peeps in at the window.

■ BELOW
A tapestry of greens in high summer, the hosta in the foreground making its mark long after the spring-flowering daphne and the peony behind have enjoyed their main period of interest.

divisions are largely a matter of individual opinion by taxonomists and it is likely that further changes in nomenclature (the system by which plants are named) will occur, since many plants grown by gardeners that were formerly considered to be true species are now known not to occur in the wild. Such plants must be of garden origin and were probably chance hybrids that occurred in gardens when hostas were first introduced and before their propensity to seed freely was known. Many names have therefore been adjusted to follow the internationally accepted conventions of nomenclature: *H. fortunei,* for instance, previously thought to be a Japanese species, is now more correctly styled as 'Fortunei', the inverted commas indicating that it is probably a hybrid of uncertain parentage.

One of the first European hosta growers of note was Empress Josephine (1763–1814) who, with her passion for exotic novelties, planted them in the garden of her country house of Malmaison. Some were exquisitely illustrated by the botanical artist Pierre Joseph Redouté (1759–1840) in his *Les Liliacées* of 1805. A later advocate of these plants in gardens was the English Victorian gardening writer Shirley Hibberd (1825–90), who developed the idea of the herbaceous border in which he suggested using hostas alongside other hardy plants including achilleas, astilbes, daylilies, geraniums (cranesbill), foxgloves, campanulas and peonies. His ideas profoundly influenced the now better-remembered Gertrude Jekyll, who was fond of combining hostas with ferns, particularly in shady courtyards.

Nevertheless, hosta breeding did not begin in earnest until the 20th

■ BELOW

H. 'Fortunei Hyacinthina' marking a turning in a path. Behind is a yellow-leaved berberis.

century and only accelerated after World War II, when interest gained ground, particularly in the USA. Hostas have never been so popular as they are today and advances in micropropagation (see Propagation) have meant that new cultivars can be brought into commerce faster than ever before. Nowadays, the range extends from plants the size of a thumbnail, suitable for troughs or rock gardens, to grand specimens that make bold statements in the border, and the variety of variegation, from bold central splashes to narrow leaf margins, seems almost infinite (for further details on leaf shapes and coloration, see The hosta plant).

Hostas as garden plants

So intense has been the interest in hybridizing and selecting during the last 40–50 years that nowadays it is probably true to say that there is a hosta for every situation, and such is the variety available that their potential in the garden is virtually unlimited. Small hostas, such as 'Blue Moon' and 'Kabitan', grow well in shaded rock gardens, and there are tiny species, such as *H. venusta,* that are happiest in troughs or sink gardens along with alpine plants. However, a typical use for the vast majority is to plant them among spring bulbs underneath deciduous trees. The unfurling hosta leaves help to disguise the unsightly fading bulb foliage and the emerging tree canopy shields the hostas from too much direct sunlight. If space is no problem, one variety planted *en masse* as ground cover in such a situation will create a soothing effect later in the season. A similarly restful effect can be created by planting hostas among spring-flowering shrubs to create a tapestry of different greens in summer when the main display has finished.

Hostas and water are natural allies and the plants will thrive in damp soil by streams and ditches. In a cool, shady site, combine them with trilliums, *Rheum alexandrae* or, provided you have acid soil, the lovely Himalayan blue poppy *Meconopsis betonicifolia. H. sieboldiana* and its cultivars will grow in sun provided the soil does not dry out, and in such a situation you could team them with astilbes, *Iris laevigata* or daylilies, *Hemerocallis.*

Very large hostas that grow into eye-catching mature plants are best treated as specimens. The urn-shaped

For an exotic look, plant your hostas with spiky phormiums and enjoy the contrast in leaf shape and texture.

■ LEFT
The aptly named 'Gold Edger' hugs the ground and makes a good edging plant.

'Krossa Regal', for instance, would look superb rising grandly from a sea of low ground-cover plants such as purple-leaved bugle (*Ajuga reptans* 'Atropurpurea'), silvery deadnettle (*Lamium maculatum* 'White Nancy' or 'Beacon Silver') or the netted leaves of *Cyclamen coum*.

An unusual and effective but often overlooked use of hostas is as an edging plant. Some, such as the aptly named 'Gold Edger', hug the ground, and have been specifically bred for that purpose.

Hostas are also superb plants for the mixed border, provided there is adequate shelter from hot sun, associating with a wide variety of plants. Blue-leaved hostas combine especially well with old roses: they provide the perfect foil for the crushed-berry tones of the gallicas and bourbons and add further lustre to the burnished pewter foliage of alba roses. In a more vibrant scheme of hot oranges, yellows and reds, the huge, simple leaves of a cultivar such as 'Green Acres', perhaps placed at the corner of the bed as a focal point or to act as a full stop, would provide the eye with a welcome resting place.

If the many variegated hostas appeal to you, try picking up the colour of variegation in flower colours. For instance, cream-edged hostas planted with the off-white *Camassia leichtlinii* or pale yellow *Roscoea cautleoides* would add flickers of light to a shaded area; yellow tulips would look good with the emerging leaves of a yellow-edged hosta such as 'Frances Williams'. It is a good idea in such situations to contrast the rounded shapes of hostas with some strong verticals, such as might be provided by foxgloves, particularly the white-flowered *Digitalis purpurea* 'Alba', *Iris foetidissima* or Japanese anemones.

Though they are primarily considered as foliage plants, do not forget that hostas also produce flowers, even if few can be called truly showy. Indeed, some gardeners feel that they add little to the hosta's beauty. Since the colour range is restricted to virtually every shade of lilac between white and purple, if you are growing the hostas with flowering plants whose colours may clash, you may prefer to remove the flower stems as they appear. Otherwise, you could combine them with plants that have

■ BELOW

A perfect marriage: hosta flowers combine well with other similarly coloured flowers, such as the border phlox shown here. The spread of the bamboo has been restricted by growing it in a container.

similarly understated flowers, such as *Nectaroscordum siculum,* the most distinguished of the onion tribe, with green- and purple-tinged white flowers, or an ornamental grass such as biscuit-coloured *Pennisetum alopecuroides* or the smaller *P.* 'Hameln' or greenish-brown *Carex pendula. En masse*, hosta flowers are perhaps best seen in light woodland, where a drift of 'Fortunei Aureo-marginata' can create much the same effect at the height of summer as bluebells do earlier in the season. Hostas flower best in sun but their leaves look best in shade so, if you want lots of flowers, you must grow them in a sunny position.

Hostas in containers

Hostas are among the most stylish of container plants, creating a lush, tropical effect unmatched by any other hardy plant. If you have only a sun-trap patio, balcony or roof garden, try the sun-loving *H. plantaginea,* but if you can provide some shade your choice among the cultivars is virtually unlimited. The advantages of growing in containers are many: you can move the plants about at will and it is much easier to control damage by slugs and snails (see Growing in containers and Hosta problems). You can thus develop flawless specimens and indulge in a little horticultural hoodwinking by dropping them into any awkward gaps that appear in your borders in mid-summer when early-flowering bulbs and perennials have shut up shop for the season.

For the grandest effect, plant large-leaved hostas in decorated terracotta, stone or lead urns, though the plants would be equally at home in wooden half-barrels or plastic containers. Use them as you would other container plants; in pairs on either side of a doorway, or to mark the start of a path or flight of steps, or as singletons at focal points. Given the affinity between hostas and water, an even number of the same

■ OPPOSITE
H. 'Summer Fragrance' in full sun grouped with ornamental grasses; a large-flowered clematis provides a touch of colour.

■ BELOW
A showy arrangement using hosta leaves to offset bold chrysanthemums and throatworts (*Trachelium caeruleum*).

variety in matching containers would look superb placed around the perimeter of a formal pool. If you want to make a display of different kinds in an informal group, growing them in similar containers of different sizes will help to create unity.

Using hostas in flower arrangements

Hosta leaves are the flower arranger's life saver, since even a few plants will provide leaves for picking from late spring to early autumn; the flowers are equally useful, when they appear. Both last well in water. The leaves are particularly effective in combination with other leaves of contrasting shape, with perhaps just a few flowers for impact (see Hostas in flower arrangements); for instance, use the huge quilted leaves of *H. sieboldiana* 'Elegans' with the spiky foliage of the Scotch thistle, *Onopordum acanthium,* possibly with a few white roses or lilies. For a more painterly effect, study the different colours on variegated leaves and apply a restricted palette of similar tones: match, for instance, a yellow-edged leaf of 'Fortunei Albopicta' with some yellow bearded irises, then add a few deeper yellows such as *Rosa* 'Maigold'. You can also use hosta leaves to flesh out arrangements that employ expensive imported or glasshouse-raised flowers from the florist, such as mimosa, *Acacia dealbata,* or even orchids. You could also use hosta leaves to create a solid base for a towering edifice comprising delphiniums, roses, irises and any other flowers in season.

The hosta plant

Hostas are hardy, clump-forming herbaceous perennials. The leaves emerge from below ground level in early spring and die back completely in autumn. They are apparently stemless but, in fact, the hosta stem has evolved into a rhizome (an underground storage organ) from which the shoots arise. In a few cases, the rhizome is stoloniferous: it grows horizontally and produces new plantlets along its length. Hostas with stoloniferous rootstocks are particularly useful as ground cover, since you do not need to divide them to create new plants.

Hosta leaves are round, oval or lance-shaped, with every gradation possible in between. In this book, the terms broadly oval and narrowly oval are used to describe the intermediate shapes. The leaves have stalks (petioles) of varying length; in some cases, as in 'Krossa Regal' and 'Green Fountain', the elongation of the petiole is distinctive and creates a plant with an overall urn shape. The base of the leaf also varies. It may be cut straight across, or wedge-shaped, or wedge-shaped with the edges concavely curved or heart-shaped with two distinct lobes on either side of the leaf stalk. Again, all manner of gradations are possible. Leaf edges may be smooth, crimped like a pie-crust or slightly wavy. In some cases, the whole leaf is twisted. Leaf surfaces vary from smooth to deeply puckered. This puckering effect, like a quilt, is most pronounced when the leaves are mature. Others have pronounced veins that are especially prominent when seen from below, giving the leaves a sculptural quality.

The substance of leaves varies from very thin to thick. Thin leaves are often glossy and shine like silk, while most thick leaves appear to

ABOVE
The scape of 'Ginko Craig'. Note the bracts behind each flower that have the same variegation as the leaves.

BELOW
A leaf of 'Krossa Regal', showing the elongated petiole.

RIGHT
An oval leaf.

ABOVE
A round leaf with a heart-shaped base.

ABOVE
A lance-shaped leaf with a glossy surface.

ABOVE AND TOP
Leaves variegated at the edge with cream and yellow.

have been dusted with a waxy bloom (pruinosity).

Leaf colours range from a bright lime green that is almost yellow to a dark blue-blackish green. Leaves may be variegated with white, cream or yellow, with the variegation appearing either as an edging to the leaf or as a bold central splash. The proportion of variegation to the main colour green in the leaf varies considerably. The more variegation, the slower the plant will be to establish, since it is the green pigment that allows photosynthesis, and thus growth, to take place.

Hostas flower from early summer onwards. The flowers are lily-like, tubular, bell-shaped or funnel-shaped and are carried normally on short, medium or tall, unbranched stems called scapes. Behind each flower is a bract that usually shares the characteristics of the main leaves but is much smaller in scale. Some hosta scapes also have a large, conspicuous bract below the lowest flower on the scape.

All hosta flowers are more or less purple, but range from very deep purple to a very pale lavender that is virtually white. A few hosta flowers are deliciously fragrant, mostly those on plants derived from the sun-loving Chinese species, *H. plantaginea.*

Hostas vary in size from tiny plants less than 10cm (4in) across to plants that will fill a cubic metre/yard or more. They form dome-shaped mounds of leaves, and even the stoloniferous kinds that make mats of foliage are made up of individual dome-shaped plantlets. Most are slow-growing, particularly the larger varieties, and take several years to achieve their full potential, when they will effectively smother any competing weeds.

BOVE
his leaf is remarkable
r the distinct thin white
ne which separates the
vo colours.

ABOVE AND LEFT
Leaves marked with central splashes.

LEFT, ABOVE AND RIGHT
Twisted leaves.

ABOVE
A leaf with a crimped, goffered or "piecrust" edge.

ABOVE
A deeply puckered or quilted leaf with pronounced veining.

Plant Catalogue

Yellow-leaved hostas

In the following gallery, hostas are arranged according to leaf colour and variegation. Hostas are described as small, medium or large, corresponding to the following measurements of the clump when fully mature (from leaf tip to opposite leaf tip): small (38cm/15in or less); medium (40–60cm/16– 24in); and large (64cm/25in or more). Plants may make larger or smaller specimens, depending on cultivation, climate, season and soil type. The dates of introduction refer to when the plant was registered. Some of the plants were grown in gardens before these dates.

■ ABOVE RIGHT

'SUN POWER'

Large hosta introduced in 1986. The large, oval to heart-shaped leaves are bright yellow-green and have wavy edges. From mid- to late summer, it produces funnel-shaped, lavender flowers on tall scapes. 'Sun Power' colours best in sun but needs some shelter to prevent leaf scorch.

■ LEFT

'GOLDEN PRAYERS'

Medium hosta introduced in 1976. The small, puckered, vivid golden yellow leaves are held erect. In mid-summer the virtually white flowers appear. 'Golden Prayers' increases quickly.

■ RIGHT

'MIDAS TOUCH'

Medium hosta introduced in 1978. The substantial, deeply puckered, heart-shaped leaves are bright yellow-green with a metallic sheen. The virtually white flowers are borne from mid- to late summer. One of the best yellow-leaved hostas, 'Midas Touch' tolerates full sun.

■ LEFT

'ZOUNDS'

Large hosta introduced in 1978. The large, heavily puckered leaves are golden yellow, developing a metallic sheen as they mature. The funnel-shaped flowers, borne in mid-summer, are pale lavender to white. A sumptuous plant, if slow to establish, 'Zounds' keeps its colour in shade better than most other yellow-leaved hostas.

■ RIGHT

'SUM AND SUBSTANCE'

Large hosta introduced in 1980. The large, substantial, puckered leaves have pointed tips and are greenish to bright yellow, depending on the degree of sun. From mid- to late summer, and sometimes later, the pale mauve flowers appear on tall scapes. 'Sum and Substance', a superb plant when mature, is justifiably one of the most popular modern hostas.

■ LEFT

'GOLD REGAL'

Large hosta introduced in 1974. The large, substantial, puckered leaves have pointed tips and are golden yellow overlaid with grey. The large, bell-shaped, pale purple flowers are carried in mid-summer. 'Gold Regal' is slow to establish and is best in sun.

■ RIGHT

'PIEDMONT GOLD'

Large hosta introduced in 1974. The large, yellowish green leaves are of a thick texture, puckered and wavy-edged, and have a distinct whitish bloom. The funnel-shaped flowers, carried in mid-summer, are pale lavender-white. 'Piedmont Gold', one of the grandest yellows, prefers more shade than most others in this group and needs several years to develop its full potential.

■ LEFT

'AUGUST MOON'

Large hosta introduced in 1968. The first leaves to appear are oval to heart-shaped, soft yellow, slightly puckered, and develop a faint greyish-blue bloom; later leaves are bright yellow. The flowers, borne in mid-summer, are pale greyish-lavender to white. A vigorous plant, 'August Moon' produces its best leaf colour in sun.

Green-leaved hostas

■ RIGHT

H. VENTRICOSA

Large species from China. The shiny green leaves are oval with pointed tips and heart-shaped bases. Striking, bell-shaped, deep violet flowers are produced in late summer. *H. ventricosa,* one of the most elegant hostas, can be propagated by seed.

■ BELOW

'GREEN ACRES'

Large hosta introduced in 1970. The large, oval leaves, held on tall petioles and tapering to a point, have heart-shaped bases and are deeply ribbed. The funnel-shaped flowers, borne from early to mid-summer, are near white. A mature specimen of 'Green Acres' makes a striking garden plant.

■ RIGHT

'TALL BOY'

Large hosta introduced in 1983. The somewhat shiny leaves are oval to heart-shaped. In mid-summer, the striking, funnel-shaped, light purple flowers are carried on unusually tall scapes. Almost uniquely in this genus, 'Tall Boy' is grown for its flowers rather than its foliage.

■ ABOVE

'HONEYBELLS'

Large hosta introduced in 1986. The large, broadly oval, glossy green leaves have slightly wavy edges. In mid- to late summer, slightly fragrant, bell-shaped, pale lilac or near white flowers are produced. 'Honeybells' is a vigorous hosta that tolerates some sun.

■ ABOVE

'DEVON GREEN'

Medium hosta introduced in 1988. The dark green, narrowly heart-shaped leaves are smooth, distinctly ribbed and shiny; the petioles are spotted with purple. The bell-shaped flowers are greyish-lavender to near white and are produced in mid-summer. 'Devon Green', an outstandingly beautiful hosta, is a sport of 'Halcyon'.

■ RIGHT

H. VENUSTA

Dwarf species from Korea. It has oval to lance-shaped leaves and, from late summer to mid-autumn, abundant scapes carrying racemes of violet flowers. *H. venusta*, the smallest species in cultivation, is suitable for a rock garden.

Blue-leaved hostas

■ RIGHT

H. NIGRESCENS

Large species from Japan. The broadly oval, puckered leaves have heart-shaped bases. The bell-shaped, virtually white flowers open from pale purple buds in late summer. *H. nigrescens*, which makes a vase-shaped clump, is known in its country of origin as the black hosta, referring to the colour of the shoots that emerge from the crown in spring.

■ ABOVE

'PEARL LAKE'

Medium hosta introduced in 1982. The small, greyish-green leaves are carried on tall petioles. In mid-summer, and sometimes again later, it produces masses of pale lavender, funnel-shaped flowers. 'Pearl Lake', which rapidly forms dense clumps, is suitable for mass planting as ground cover.

■ OPPOSITE

'KROSSA REGAL'

Large hosta introduced in 1980. The large, substantial, slightly wavy-edged leaves are bluish-green with a waxy bloom and are carried on tall petioles, making a handsome, urn-shaped plant. In mid-summer, funnel-shaped lavender flowers appear. 'Krossa Regal' tolerates some sun, but at the expense of the best leaf colour.

■ BELOW

'BLUE MOON'

Small hosta introduced in 1976. The thick puckered leaves are round to heart-shaped, and glaucous dark blue. The bell-shaped flowers are pale lavender to white. 'Blue Moon' is suitable for a rock garden.

■ ABOVE

'BLUE CADET'

Small hosta introduced in 1974. The thick puckered leaves, which are nearly round and have pointed tips, are intensely glaucous blue. The purple flowers appear in mid-summer. 'Blue Cadet' is one of the most outstanding, small, blue-leaved hostas.

■ OPPOSITE BELOW

'HADSPEN BLUE'

Medium hosta introduced in 1988. The substantial leaves are heart-shaped and intensely glaucous blue. In mid-summer, the bell-shaped lavender flowers appear on upright scapes just overtopping the leaf mould. 'Hadspen Blue' is similar to 'Halcyon' but is rather smaller; mature plants have the best leaf colour.

■ ABOVE

'BLUE ANGEL'

Large hosta introduced in 1986. The huge, heart-shaped, glaucous blue-grey leaves are thick and less puckered than most of this type. Very pale mauve to white flowers are borne from mid- to late summer. 'Blue Angel' is slow to establish but is one of the most impressive of its type.

■ RIGHT

'HALCYON'

Medium hosta introduced in 1988. The substantial, intensely blue leaves, oval on emergence, mature to a heart shape. In mid-summer, the near white flowers are held on upright scapes which just top the leaf mould. 'Halcyon' is a superb hosta for a container.

■ RIGHT

'BLUE WEDGWOOD'

Medium hosta introduced in 1988. The thick, heavily puckered, intensely glaucous blue leaves have wavy margins. In mid-summer, pale lavender to white, bell-shaped flowers are borne. 'Blue Wedgwood', one of the bluest hostas, makes an elegant, shapely plant.

■ OPPOSITE

'LOVE PAT'

Medium or large hosta introduced in 1978. The substantial round leaves are deeply puckered and are intensely glaucous blue. In mid-summer, the pale lilac or near white flowers are carried on upright scapes. 'Love Pat' derives from 'Tokudama' (formerly *H. tokudama*) but is larger and more vigorous.

■ BELOW

'HADSPEN HERON'

Small hosta introduced in 1976. The substantial leaves are oval to lance-shaped and glaucous blue-green. In mid-summer, the bell-shaped, near white flowers appear. The leaf shape of 'Hadspen Heron' is unique among the "blue" hostas.

■ ABOVE

H. SIEBOLDIANA 'ELEGANS'

Large hosta introduced in 1954. The very large, substantial leaves are deeply puckered and are intensely glaucous blue-green. From early to mid-summer, the virtually white flowers appear among the leaves on upright scapes. A superb plant when fully mature, *H. sieboldiana* 'Elegans' has one of the most impressive track records of any of the "blues".

Variegated chartreuse-yellow-leaved hostas

■ ABOVE

'SHADE FANFARE'

Medium hosta introduced in 1986. The yellowish-green, heart-shaped leaves are broadly margined with creamy white. The lavender flowers are freely produced in mid-summer. 'Shade Fanfare' is one of the best of all variegated hostas; in sun, the leaves are bright golden yellow with white margins.

Variegated green-leaved hostas

■ LEFT

H. VENTRICOSA 'VARIEGATA'

Large hosta first described in 1876 and later apparently lost to cultivation until the mid-20th century. The oval leaves, heart-shaped at the base and with a satin-like sheen, are streaked and margined with creamy white. Bell-shaped, deep purple flowers appear on tall scapes in late summer. One of the oldest variegated hostas, *H. ventricosa* 'Variegata' remains one of the best.

■ BELOW

'FRANCEE'

Large hosta introduced in 1986. The large leaves are oval to heart-shaped and are narrowly edged with white. The funnel-shaped flowers, produced in mid-summer, are lavender-purple. 'Francee' is effective in a shady corner and is also a good subject for containers.

■ BELOW

H. SIEBOLDII

Small species from Japan. The narrowly oval or lance-shaped leaves have white margins and slightly wavy edges. Pale mauve flowers streaked with violet appear from late summer to early autumn. *H. sieboldii* is one of the most widely distributed hostas in the wild.

■ ABOVE

'ANTIOCH'

Large hosta introduced in 1979. The oval leaves, irregularly margined with cream or creamy white, taper to a point. In mid-summer, the funnel-shaped lavender flowers appear. An elegant plant, 'Antioch' grows best in rich soil in full shade.

■ RIGHT

'WIDE BRIM'

Medium hosta introduced in 1979. The substantial heart-shaped leaves are puckered, slightly tinged blue, and broadly edged with creamy white. The funnel-shaped, virtually white flowers are carried on erect scapes in mid-summer. An established plant of 'Wide Brim' is an impressive sight.

■ RIGHT
'GINKO CRAIG'

Small or medium hosta introduced in 1986. The lance-shaped, wavy-edged leaves are crisply margined with white. The funnel-shaped, deep mauve flowers are freely produced in mid-summer. 'Ginko Craig' makes a good edging plant.

■ RIGHT

'BRIM CUP'

Small hosta introduced in 1986. The small, round to heart-shaped leaves develop puckering as they age and are broadly edged with creamy white. The bell-shaped, pale lavender to white flowers are produced in mid-summer. 'Brim Cup' derives from the much larger 'Wide Brim'.

■ RIGHT

'GOLDEN TIARA'

Small hosta introduced in 1977. The small, oval to round leaves have creamy yellow edges that deepen to greenish-yellow as they mature. The tall, erect scapes carry striking, bell-shaped, lavender-purple flowers with white throats in mid-summer, and sometimes again later. 'Golden Tiara' makes a neat-growing, compact plant.

■ LEFT

'BOLD RIBBONS'

Medium hosta introduced in 1976. The olive-green, narrowly oval leaves have distinct but irregular cream or creamy white margins. The rich purple flowers are produced in mid-summer. As 'Bold Ribbons' spreads by stolons it is not suitable for growing in containers.

Variegated blue-leaved hostas

■ LEFT

'TOKUDAMA FLAVOCIRCINALIS'

Medium hosta introduced in 1940. The substantial, broadly oval to round leaves are deeply puckered and have irregular yellowish-green or yellow margins. The virtually white, bell-shaped flowers are produced on erect scapes in mid-summer. 'Tokudama Flavocircinalis' is similar to 'Frances Williams' but makes a smaller plant.

■ OPPOSITE

'FRANCES WILLIAMS'

Large hosta introduced in 1936. The large, substantial, puckered leaves are round or heart-shaped and are deep glaucous blue irregularly edged with creamy beige. In mid-summer, the large, pale lavender-white flowers appear in dense racemes. 'Frances Williams', named after the great hosta grower who discovered it as a sport of *H. sieboldiana* 'Elegans', is justifiably one of the most popular of all hostas.

■ LEFT

H. FLUCTUANS 'SAGAE'

Large hosta, sometimes known as *H. fluctuans* 'Variegated', introduced in 1985. The huge, thick leaves have long, upright petioles; they are margined with cream or creamy yellow and the edges are gently wavy. The funnel-shaped flowers, borne in mid-summer, are pale lavender overlaid with purple. Bred in Japan, *H. fluctuans* 'Sagae' is one of the most dramatic and desirable of all hostas.

Hostas with centrally splashed leaves

■ ABOVE

'JUNE'

Medium hosta introduced in 1991. The substantial leaves are oval to lance-shaped as they emerge, becoming rounder as they develop. Bluish-green, they have a central strong yellow splash that darkens to greenish-yellow as the season advances. Bell-shaped, near white flowers are produced on erect scapes in mid-summer. 'June', a sport of 'Halcyon', is one of the most outstanding of the modern introductions.

■ OPPOSITE BELOW

'GOLD STANDARD'

Large hosta introduced in 1976. The large, heart-shaped leaves are generously splashed with greenish-yellow that becomes a brighter yellow as they develop before fading to buff-beige. The funnel-shaped flowers are carried on erect scapes in mid-summer. Site 'Gold Standard' with care: too much sun and the leaves burn; not enough, and they fail to develop their best colour, turning green in too much shade.

■ ABOVE LEFT

'UNDULATA UNIVITTATA'

Medium hosta, a form of 'Undulata' (see below). The glossy green leaves have a central ivory white stripe. In early to mid-summer, the lavender flowers appear. Plants of this form are slightly larger and more vigorous than 'Undulata' owing to the greater amount of green in the leaf.

■ ABOVE RIGHT

'UNDULATA'

Medium hosta introduced in 1797. The twisted, wavy-edged leaves are centrally splashed with creamy white. The lavender flowers are carried on erect scapes from early to mid-summer. 'Undulata' is a beautiful but unstable hosta; the first flush of leaves have the most white, later leaves have more green streaks. As the clump ages, each year it produces leaves that are progressively more green and less twisted with straighter edges. Plants with leaves that have merely a central ivory stripe are sold as 'Undulata Univittata' (see above). To maintain the desired form, therefore, divide the clump every three years, otherwise it will revert in time to plain green.

Cultivation of hostas

Hostas will grow in all soils apart from very chalky or boggy soil, but generally prefer one that is heavy and slightly acid. Very small hostas tolerate quite poor soils and are best in raised beds or in rock gardens, but most others are greedy plants that demand a high level of soil fertility. In general, the bigger the hosta the greater the need for good-quality soil.

Soil fertility can be improved by adding organic matter such as garden compost, well-rotted farmyard manure or spent mushroom compost. These also improve the soil structure by opening up heavy clay and thus improving drainage and, conversely, by forming sponge-like crumbs that help retain moisture in light, free-draining soil. If you have very heavy soil, improve the drainage by working in a bucketful of horticultural grit to every square metre/yard.

Shade is important for all hostas, apart from *H. plantaginea* and its hybrids, which need full sun. As a rule of thumb, the thinner the leaf the greater the need for shade, since thin leaves are more prone to scorch. The ideal light level for most hostas is the light dappled shade under deciduous trees. Some will tolerate full sun, though with thick-leaved varieties this may be to the detriment of the bloom on the leaf, and hence leaf colour will not be so intense. A position that receives some sun (though not at midday) is necessary

IMPROVING THE SOIL

1 Fork over the site to break up and aerate the soil.

2 Remove all weeds, particularly perennials such as ground elder and couch grass.

3 Fork in organic matter at about the rate of one bucketful per square metre/yard.

■ RIGHT
In this subtle scheme, the old gold variegation of 'Frances Williams' is the brightest element in a planting that includes shade-loving hellebores and ferns.

HOSTAS THAT TOLERATE SUN

Apart from H. plantaginea *and 'Aphrodite', the following need to be shaded from hot summer sun.*

- 'Aphrodite'
- 'August Moon'
- 'Blonde Elf'
- 'Fortunei Aureomarginata'
- 'Fragrant Gold'
- 'Gold Drop'
- 'Gold Regal'
- 'Golden Medallion'
- 'Honeybells'
- *H. hypoleuca*
- 'June'
- 'Little Aurora'
- 'Marilyn'
- 'Midas Touch'
- *H. plantaginea* and forms
- 'Royal Standard'
- 'Sea Drift'
- 'Shining Tot'
- *H. sieboldii*
- 'Snow Cap'
- 'So Sweet'
- 'Sugar and Cream'
- 'Sultana'
- 'Sum and Substance'
- 'Sweet Susan'
- 'Vanilla Cream'
- 'Vera Verde'
- *H. yingeri*

to enhance the variegation of those with variegated foliage, though yellow markings will fade to cream or even white with too much sun. Some sun is also necessary for yellow-leaved hostas that turn mid-green in shade. Green-leaved hostas will grow in quite deep shade. Hostas flower more freely in sun, though the flowers will last longer and hold their colour better in shade. You may need to move plants several times before you find the ideal position for them.

Some shelter from wind is desirable since excessive wind can scorch the leaves. Planting hostas among shrubs and/or other taller-growing perennials usually ensures adequate protection.

Mulches

Peat improves soil texture but is inert and does not provide any additional nutrients. Conservationists often frown on its use in the garden, since it is not a renewable resource.

Spent mushroom compost is an excellent mulching material but as it is usually alkaline it is unsuitable for use on soils that are already very limy.

Crushed cocoa shell is pleasant to handle and is sometimes claimed to deter slugs and snails, but being light and dry it tends to blow about in windy weather.

Worm compost, made by introducing composting worms into a bin containing vegetable waste, is a superb mulching material high in nutrients, but it needs to be made in a controlled environment.

Mulching and feeding

Hostas should be mulched in autumn and spring, by spreading a doughnut-like ring of organic matter around the crown of the plant. For optimum results, you should additionally feed while the plants are in growth from spring onwards. For the best leaves, apply a high-nitrogen feed in early spring in the form of dried blood, pelleted chicken manure or a proprietary chemical fertilizer, but excessive nitrogen later in the season will lead to over-lush growth that is susceptible to disease. Potassium helps to firm the growth and improves flowering, so from late

Mulching

1 Clear any debris or fallen leaves from around the plant. Before mulching, apply slug pellets around the base of the plant, following the manufacturer's instructions.

2 Spread a layer of organic matter, at least 10cm (4in) thick, in a doughnut-like ring around the crown of the plant.

3 Replace the mulch at the end of the growing season or at the beginning of the next growing season. If you are using a wet mulch, it should not touch the leaves, or rotting could result.

spring to mid-summer switch to a high-potash fertilizer, such as a rose or tomato feed. In autumn, a dressing of bonemeal that is high in phosphorus will benefit root growth. You can achieve good results, however, by using a balanced (or "straight") fertilizer that contains the major elements in equal amounts throughout the season. When using any fertilizer, always follow the manufacturer's instructions.

Watering

Strictly speaking, a plant that has been properly planted and mulched should not need additional watering during the growing season; indeed, periods of drought can be beneficial to plants, stimulating the roots to grow downwards in search of moisture even though the top-growth may suffer temporarily. But if you cannot bear the sight of wilting leaves at the height of summer, additional watering will be necessary. In general, the less shade you provide the more you are likely to need to water, since soil dries out more quickly in full sun. Watering is best carried out in the early morning, not early evening as is often recommended for other plants, since this will encourage slugs and snails.

To check that the roots of a plant are not congested, ease the plant out of its container. To do this, turn the plant upside down and gently knock the side of the pot against a hard surface in order to loosen the plant.

A hosta showing leaves eaten by slugs and snails. In this case the damage is not seriously detrimental, but you should avoid buying plants that have been heavily attacked.

Water thoroughly around the base of the plant. Wetting the leaves can result in scorch if the plants are in full sun, and can also leave unsightly blotches and spoil any bloom as the excess moisture evaporates. If you have a large number of hostas, the ideal method is an overhead watering system that releases the water as a mist or as tiny droplets to simulate the conditions in which most hostas grow in the wild, but this would be expensive to install and is for dedicated growers only.

Buying a hosta

When buying hostas, look for healthy, strong-growing specimens that have not been subject to attack from slugs or snails. Where feasible, ease the plant from its pot to check that it is not pot-bound. Reject any plant that has congested roots that are tightly coiled around the inside of the pot. They will continue to grow in a spiral, and the plant will be slow to establish. Large plants will establish more quickly than small ones.

Hostas are occasionally available in early spring as bare-root plants in perforated polythene bags. These should be soaked in water for about an hour prior to planting.

Planting a hosta

Hostas are best planted in spring or autumn, but can also be planted when in full growth provided they are kept well watered after planting. The fertility of the soil should first be improved (see Cultivation of hostas).

When planting, set the crowns below the soil surface to minimize the risk of the roots drying out. After planting, water well and apply a thick mulch of organic matter (see feature box on Mulches).

All hostas are subject to damage by slugs and snails, particularly in the early stages of growth, and you will almost certainly need to take preventative measures when you plant a hosta (see Hosta problems).

1 Prepare the soil, then dig a hole roughly twice the width and depth of the pot.

2 Slide the hosta from its pot and place in the hole to check the planting depth. Lay a cane across the hole to determine soil level. Aim to plant the hosta about 2.5cm (1in) deeper than it was in the container.

3 Backfill with soil and firm the hosta in with your hands, then water in thoroughly.

4 Apply slug pellets at the rate recommended by the manufacturer.

5 *(left)* Mulch with organic matter – mushroom compost was used here. Make sure that the mulch does not touch the leaves since this could lead to rotting.

■ BELOW
Hosta 'Sugar and Cream' will increase rapidly, given good cultivation.

Cutting down

If you are planting in summer, cut down some or all of the leaves to prevent excessive moisture loss from the leaf surfaces.

1 Spread the leaves of the hosta with your hand and, with a sharp knife, cut them back close to the crown.

2 Cutting down helps a hosta planted in the summer to establish; fresh leaves may appear later in the season.

Growing in containers

Hostas thrive in containers. If you have a serious problem with slugs and snails, this is often the most practical way of growing them. Many of these pests seem to resent the climb up the sides of the pots and will probably leave your plants in peace, but if any do appear it is easy to remove them by hand before they have done too much damage, a procedure that is often impractical where hostas are grown in a large border among other plants.

1 Fill the base of the pot with crocks to a depth of 2.5–5cm (1–2in) for drainage.

2 Begin to fill the pot with your choice of compost.

3 Wearing gloves, fork in a handful or two of bonemeal or other type of slow-release fertilizer.

4 Add a little compost and sit the hosta on top. Check that, when planted, there will be a gap of approximately 2.5cm (1in) between the rim of the container and the top of the compost to allow for generous watering.

5 Remove the hosta from its pot and gently fork over the rootball to free the roots. This will help the plant to establish quickly, but do not damage the roots.

On the patio or terrace, hostas in pots can look stunning if arranged in groups, but site them with care. A position in full sun at the height of summer may bake the roots and scorch the leaves, so move them into shade on hot days. Choose a container that will accommodate the growth you expect the plant to achieve during the growing season.

Hostas in containers need regular watering. Apply the water below the leaf canopy and around the crown rather than over the leaves since excessive wetting can leave unsightly

6 Centre the hosta in the pot and backfill with more compost.

7 Water the container thoroughly after planting.

8 Cover the surface of the compost with a thick layer of horticultural grit. This will deter slugs and snails and help to keep the roots cool, as well as preventing the surface of the compost from drying out too quickly.

marks, particularly if your water is very alkaline. If you live in a hard-water area, therefore, use rainwater collected in a waterbutt. Alternatively, install a water softener to minimize the risk.

Nutrients in proprietary composts are rapidly exhausted (after about 6–8 weeks), so you will also need to feed your plants. Use a liquid feed and follow the regime suggested in Cultivation of hostas. You do not need to repot your hostas every year unless you are troubled by the vine weevil (see Hosta problems). Many hostas will grow adequately in the same container for up to four years, gradually increasing in bulk and producing larger leaves. However, you should top-dress the plants annually in spring. To do this, tilt the pot and scrape out the top 2.5cm (1in) of compost with your fingers, replace with fresh compost and then

■ LEFT
Hostas in containers grouped with the tender Australian tree fern (*Dicksonia antarctica*) around a bubble fountain.

COMPOSTS

Choice of compost is a personal matter. Loamless composts are light and easy to handle, but can become waterlogged and stagnant if you overwater; conversely, if allowed to dry out, they are difficult to rewet. Loam-based types, though more expensive, do not have these drawbacks and are preferable provided the extra weight is not a problem. If you decide to use a loam-based type, John Innes No. 2 is the appropriate formula. Bearing in mind that hostas are woodland plants, you can replace up to half the compost with leaf mould or garden compost. For small-leaved rock garden types, work a handful or two of horticultural grit into the compost to help drainage.

■ BELOW
An outstandingly elegant hosta, 'Green Fountain' makes a splendid choice for a container.

fork in a little slow-release fertilizer. When the plants become congested, remove the clumps from the pots and divide them (see Propagation). Return some of the pieces to the same pot using fresh compost or pot them up individually.

HOSTAS THAT THRIVE IN CONTAINERS

Most are suitable, the following being particularly recommended.

- 'Candy Hearts'
- 'Celebration'
- 'Francee'
- 'Gold Standard'
- 'Golden Prayers'
- 'Green Fountain'
- 'Halcyon'
- 'Happy Hearts'
- 'Iona'
- 'June'
- 'Krossa Regal'
- 'Lancifolia'
- 'Masquerade'
- 'Pastures New'
- *H. plantaginea* and forms
- 'Shade Fanfare'
- 'Shining Tot'
- 'Snowden'
- 'Spritzer'
- 'Wide Brim'

Propagation

1 This hosta is congested: the emerging shoots are tightly packed and the plant has started to encroach on its neighbours.

2 Lift the whole clump, using a garden fork, and carry it to a place where you can work comfortably.

3 Using a sharp garden knife, cut up the clump piece by piece.

Propagating hostas is a straightforward procedure: no complicated techniques are involved. Simple division is the best way of increasing your stocks but should only be used on mature, established plants, since the divisions will take a season or two to recover. Once you have split a plant, it is wisest to let it grow on undisturbed for at least three years, preferably longer, before dividing it again. To get round this problem, professional nurserymen use a technique known as micro-propagation, which is the quickest way of producing large stocks of new cultivars. Tiny pieces of the parent plant are rooted in laboratory conditions then grown on under cover. Since the growing environment has to be kept sterile at all times, this is obviously a technique that is beyond the amateur gardener.

4 Make clean cuts, ensuring that each division has a good root system.

5 An alternative method is to push two forks back-to-back into the clump, then prise them apart. Whichever method you use, carry on until you have split the whole clump into even-sized pieces.

6 Replant the best pieces, and fill in with fresh soil from another part of the garden.

7 Firm the pieces in with your hands. Water them in thoroughly. The remaining divisions can either be planted out elsewhere, potted up for replanting later in the garden or, as container plants, given to friends, or composted.

Hostas can be divided in several ways: either dig up the clump and cut it up into single crowns with roots, using a sharp knife, or split it using two garden forks held back-to-back as levers. A further method is to take a wedge out of an established clump, rather as one would a slice from a circular cake, and use that as a new plant, re-filling the hole with good compost. Another option, if your soil is very light, is simply to pull the hosta apart into pieces with your hands, but watch out for sharp stones that may be entwined in the roots.

Spring, when the shoots are emerging, is the best time for dividing, as the plants then have the rest of the growing season in which to recover, but you can also divide them in autumn, when the leaves have died down. You should always divide hostas when they become congested; this is greatly to their benefit.

RAISING HOSTAS FROM SEED

Hostas can also be raised from seed, but the seedlings vary greatly in quality and few are likely either to resemble the parent or even to make good garden plants. Nevertheless, if you wish to try this method, gather the seed when ripe in autumn. Sow it in trays of seed compost, then overwinter them in a cold frame outdoors. The seed should germinate by the following spring. When the seedlings are large enough to handle, prick them out into pots and grow them on in an open frame. They should be large enough to plant out the following spring.

Hosta problems

Slugs and snails

On the whole, hostas are very healthy plants that, given good cultivation, are generally free of pests and diseases. However, you are likely to encounter problems with slugs and snails eating holes in the leaves, and there are few situations in which some form of control is unnecessary. The conditions that suit most hostas – cool, damp shade – are also those in which the molluscs thrive.

Young hosta leaves are most attractive to slugs and unfortunately any damage done at this stage stays visible throughout the season, so you need to begin slug control early. Hostas with thick leaves are less appealing to slugs and snails; those with very thin leaves are most vulnerable.

You should aim to keep down the numbers of slugs and snails in the garden by not creating the habitats in which they can increase. Remove all rotting vegetation and other debris from the soil as a matter of course, particularly in autumn, since the molluscs lay their eggs among dead leaves to overwinter. Keep the site clear of large stones and bricks that will harbour the pests on their undersides. If you grow hostas in containers, regularly check their bases and remove any slugs you find there. Birds, frogs, toads and hedgehogs prey on slugs and snails, so you

HOSTAS RESISTANT TO SLUGS AND SNAILS

While no hosta is fully resistant to attack from slugs and snails, the following are less palatable to these pests than most.

- 'Big Daddy'
- 'El Capitan'
- 'Frances Williams'
- 'Fringe Benefit'
- 'Golden Bullion'
- 'Invincible'
- 'Krossa Regal'
- *H. rupifraga*
- 'Sea Drift'
- 'Silvery Slugproof'
- 'Sum and Substance'
- 'Tardiflora'

When slugs and snails eat holes in hosta leaves they will remain visible throughout the growing season.

A mulch of horticultural grit can deter slugs and snails.

A saucer of beer placed near a hosta will lure slugs and snails to a bibulous death.

should encourage them into the garden, if possible.

Certain mulches can also deter the molluscs. A thick layer of sharp-edged horticultural grit around the plants provides a surface that they may find difficult to negotiate; crushed cocoa shell is also believed to be unattractive to them.

There are various methods of poisoning slugs and snails. One is to water liquid metaldehyde around the plants as the leaves emerge in early spring, repeating the treatment for about six to eight weeks. Slug pellets are more popular, however, since they are easy to handle. The pellets are usually blue, a colour that is reckoned to be unattractive to birds. Some contain repellents to deter domestic pets from eating them. They should be applied regularly beneath any mulch, since this is where the pests will be active, and are only effective when the soil is wet. Use them sparingly, at the rate recommended by the manufacturer. They contain a chemical which attracts slugs and snails, but if used too liberally may attract these pests into your garden.

Slug pellets provide effective control, though their use is sometimes frowned upon by the ecologically minded.

If you prefer not to use poisons in the garden, the most effective method of control is to patrol the garden with a torch at night when the slugs and snails are active. Pick them off by hand and dispose of them. Inspect the plants as well as the surrounding soil, since many small species hide among the leaves themselves. Slug pubs – saucers of beer sunk in the ground around the plants – can trap the pests, but they do not look very attractive.

Biological control is available in the form of a parasitic nematode that the slugs ingest. The nematode is usually supplied by mail order and is applied in solution, watered around the plants in early spring. This is probably the most reliable biological method, but it is also the most expensive and does not necessarily control snails.

Viruses

Hostas are occasionally subject to viruses, usually apparent as a yellowing in blotches on the leaf surface (mosaic virus); sometimes the whole leaf turns yellow. Dig up and burn any affected plants to prevent the spread of the virus.

Hostas in containers are susceptible to attack by the vine weevil, a flightless beetle that lays its eggs on the surface of the compost. The adult beetles eat leaves, but worse damage is caused by the creamy white larvae that in winter and early spring attack the roots of plants and thus are seldom seen. If top-growth slows down or stops altogether, remove the plant from the pot and check for the presence of larvae. Badly damaged plants will not recover and should be destroyed, but you will need to take preventive measures to ensure that your other plants are not affected. Applying species of the parasitic nematode *Heterorhabditis* in solution as a root drench is an effective method of control. Where the pest is prevalent, you should repot your hostas annually. Remove the plant from its pot, wash the root system free of all old compost and check it for signs of infestation, then repot.

Hostas in flower arrangements

Preparing the material

Hosta leaves and flowers for arranging are best picked early in the morning. After a cool night, plant tissues are more turgid, having absorbed overnight dew. For the benefit of the plant, and to increase your options when arranging, cut the leaves and flowers with as long a stem as possible. This avoids leaving an unsightly length of stem on the plant that will wither and may become a source of infection. If you are planning to use florist's foam, cut the stems on the slant to make them easier to insert. Use sharp scissors, secateurs or a knife, particularly when gathering mature leaves, since the stems are often quite thick.

In order to ensure that your arrangements last as long as possible, you need to prepare the material properly. Plunge the leaves into water as soon as you have picked them. Tender young leaves picked in spring should be totally immersed in a bowl of water. Hold them down flat with your hands for a minute or longer until they absorb water and float just below the surface. Treated in this way, they remain plump and fresh for longer after arranging. Mature leaves cut from mid-summer onwards can

1 Look for unblemished leaves of regular shape. Reach well inside the hosta and cut the leaves as near to the crown as possible. Cut the stem on the slant if you are intending to use florist's foam.

2 Immerse young leaves in water, holding them down for a couple of minutes until they have absorbed sufficient water to float just below the surface.

3 Stand mature leaves in the deepest possible water.

4 Spreading the leaves with your hands for easy access, cut hosta flowers with as long a stem as possible.

■ LEFT
A striking combination of hosta leaves with exotic-looking flowers such as nerines.

be stood upright in the deepest possible water until you need them for arranging.

After this treatment, hosta leaves last a long time in an arrangement, far outliving any flowers you use: as the flowers fade, you can replace them with fresh ones, leaving the hosta leaves in place. They will continue to look very attractive even as they begin to fade. An arrangement can last for several weeks, therefore, and you can ring the changes by using different flower material.

Using hosta leaves

Part of the value of using hosta leaves is that they blend with virtually anything. Remember that texture is important, too: some hosta leaves are very dainty and delicate looking, while others are more robust. The latter are perhaps better suited to large flowers. Use the thick, glaucous leaves of, for instance, *H. sieboldiana* or 'Frances Williams' with large flowers like peonies, roses or dahlias and use thinner, shining leaves with more delicate flowers such as irises, sweet peas (*Lathyrus odorata*), or carnations (*Dianthus*).

For a strong, eye-catching look, use complementary colours: red and green, orange and blue, yellow and violet. For a more subtle look, use

HOSTAS FOR FLOWER ARRANGEMENTS

Nearly all are suitable, the following being among the most effective and long-lasting

- 'Blue Piecrust'
- 'Fortunei Aureomarginata'
- 'Golden Sunburst'
- 'Granary Gold'
- 'Krossa Regal'
- 'Nakaimo'
- 'Sea Drift'
- 'Shade Fanfare'
- *H. sieboldiana* 'Elegans'
- 'Tall Boy'
- 'Undulata Univittata'
- 'Wide Brim'
- 'Yellow Splash Rim'

FLOWER ARRANGING

1 Decide on the basic outline of your arrangement. A roughly triangular shape is easiest. After soaking, place the block of florist's foam in a suitable container. Create a strong upright at the back of the arrangement, using either spiky iris leaves (as here) or something similar, such as *Crocosmia.* Spread out the hosta leaves to determine the best placement, then insert them into the foam.

2 Add the main flowers, shortening the stems as necessary. Here, orange Peruvian lilies *(Alstroemeria)* were combined with annual white tobacco flowers *(Nicotiana)* and salvias.

3 Fill in and soften the outline with lady's mantle and gypsophila. The flowers should remain fresh-looking for a week or more, after which they may be replaced with newly cut flowers, leaving the hosta leaves *in situ.*

pastel tones of these colours. For a restful scheme, use different tones of the same colour.

If you want the hosta leaves to be a really strong element of the design, analyse and exploit the leaf colour. If the dominant pigment is blue, a colour sometimes described as "glaucous", add some grey foliage, perhaps of contrasting form, then set a few orange flowers at the heart of the arrangement. So-called "yellow" leaves (actually bright lime green) can be enhanced by adding a few stems of similarly coloured, frothy lady's mantle (*Alchemilla mollis*).

Remember that simple arrangements are often the most effective. If you are new to flower arranging, follow a few basic guidelines. Arrangements that are roughly triangular in outline are always sympathetic and pleasing to the eye. As you gain confidence, you will probably try less regular shapes.

■ BOTTOM
'Fortunei Aureomarginata' is an excellent hosta for flower arrangements.

■ BELOW
Hosta leaves used with roses, Peruvian lilies and clematis seedheads form a tasteful centrepiece.

Use only a few flowers and stick to one or two colours. Here we used a few late garden flowers with the leaves of 'Krossa Regal'. Establish a basic framework first, then fill in with your chosen flowers. Remember you do not need a lot of different material to make an impact. Too many flowers may conflict and compete against each other, creating a restless effect. If you need to shorten stems, cut off a little at a time until you achieve the length you want.

If you are arranging in water, add a proprietary cut-flower food. Top up the water regularly. If you are using florist's foam, soak this in water for about an hour before starting your arrangement. You can keep the arrangement fresh by spraying it periodically with tepid water. This is particularly important in a hot, dry atmosphere.

In the arrangement shown on the previous page, for which florist's foam was used, the hosta leaves make a solid base for a roughly triangular design. A few stems cut from garden plants provide the main interest, then these are fleshed out with lady's mantle and gypsophila. Other similar plants would, of course, be just as effective.

Calendar

Early spring

Clear any plant debris that may harbour overwintering slug and snail eggs away from emerging shoots. Apply a high-nitrogen fertilizer (dried blood, pelleted chicken manure or a proprietary chemical fertilizer). Begin slug and snail control. Mulch with organic matter. Plant new stock, improving the soil first.

Mid-spring

Divide congested clumps and any other hostas if you wish to increase your stock. Continue to plant new stock and to control slugs and snails. Repot or top-dress hostas in containers and feed with a high-nitrogen fertilizer.

Late spring

Water, in the morning, during periods of drought. Feed with a high-potassium fertilizer and continue to control slugs and snails.

Summer

Water, in the morning, during periods of drought (water hostas in containers daily). Feed with a high-potassium fertilizer and continue to control slugs and snails. If planting new stock, cut down all or some of the top-growth. Move hostas in containers in full sun into shade on hot days.

Autumn

Gather seed of species, if required for propagation. Remove faded foliage and flowers, top-dress with bone-meal, then apply a mulch of organic matter. Plant new stock, improving the soil first. Divide congested clumps and any other hostas if you wish to increase your stock.

Other recommended hostas

Besides the hostas illustrated in the Plant Catalogue the following are also recommended. The date given in parentheses after each name is the date of introduction or registration, where this is known.

'Aphrodite' (1940) Large hosta with heart-shaped green leaves and double, fragrant, near white flowers. A sport of *H. plantaginea*.

'Bees Colossus' Large hosta with oval green leaves, heart-shaped at the base, and pale lavender flowers. Makes a huge mound in a shady position.

'Big Daddy' (1978) Large hosta with near round, puckered, glaucous blue leaves and near white flowers. Slow to establish.

'Birchwood Parky's Gold' (1986) Small hosta with heart-shaped, yellowish-green leaves and lavender flowers. Best with some shade.

'Blonde Elf' Medium hosta with lance-shaped, greenish-yellow leaves and masses of lavender flowers. Suits a rock garden.

'Blue Boy'

'Blue Boy' Medium hosta with glaucous blue-green leaves and pale lavender flowers. Good with *Dicentra spectabilis*.

'Blue Piecrust' (1986) Large hosta with heart-shaped, glaucous blue leaves that are ruffled at the edges and virtually white flowers. Good in flower arrangements.

'Blue Umbrellas' (1978) Large hosta with substantial glaucous blue leaves that curve downwards – hence the name – and near white flowers. Tolerates sun where the soil does not dry out.
'Bright Lights' Small or medium hosta with blue leaves splashed with yellow, and pale lavender or near white flowers. Similar to 'Tokudama Aureonebulosa' but more vigorous.
'Buckshaw Blue' (1986) Medium hosta with heart-shaped, glaucous bluish-green leaves and lavender or near white flowers. A good "blue" hosta.
'Candy Hearts' (1971) Small or medium hosta with heart-shaped, glaucous greyish-green leaves and virtually white flowers. Good in a container.
'Carol'(1986) Large hosta with oval green leaves that have white edges and a glaucous bloom, and lavender flowers. Similar to 'Francee' but less vigorous.
'Celebration' (1978) Small or medium hosta with dark green leaves splashed with creamy white, and deep lavender flowers. Subject to frost damage in cold climates.
'Chinese Sunrise' Small or medium hosta with lance-shaped, dark green leaves splashed with greenish-yellow and masses of purple flowers. Outstandingly beautiful.
'Christmas Tree' (1982) Large hosta with heart-shaped green leaves edged with creamy white, and lavender flowers. A striking plant.
'Crispula' (1940) Large hosta with broadly oval, dark green leaves margined with white and pale lavender flowers. Susceptible to viruses.
'Decorata' (1930) Medium to large hosta with broadly oval, mid-green leaves edged with white and purple flowers. Good for woodland planting.
'Devon Blue' (1988) Medium hosta with oval to heart-shaped, glaucous bluish-green leaves and lavender flowers. A "blue" hosta of merit.
'El Capitan' (1987) Medium hosta with oval to heart-shaped, glaucous green leaves that are margined yellow and lavender flowers. Resists slugs and snails.
'Elisabeth' (1983) Small to medium hosta with oval, mid-green leaves that have crimped edges and purple flowers. Of German origin.
'Fortunei Aureomarginata' (1931) Large hosta with oval to heart-shaped, mid-green leaves edged with creamy yellow and violet flowers. Is good for mass planting.
'Fortunei Hyacinthina' (1954) Large hosta with oval to heart-shaped, glaucous grey-green leaves and pale lilac flowers. Considered one of the best hostas for flowers.
'Fragrant Gold' (1982) Large hosta with oval to heart-shaped, puckered, greenish-gold leaves and slightly fragrant, lavender flowers.

'Colossal'

'Frosted Jade' (1978) Large hosta with oval, slightly wavy-edged, greyish-green leaves margined with white and virtually white flowers.
'Gold Drop' (1977) Small hosta with heart-shaped, greenish-yellow leaves and near white flowers. Best leaf colour with some sun.
'Golden Bullion' (1989) Small to medium hosta with oval to heart-shaped, puckered, greenish-yellow leaves and pale lavender flowers. Resists slugs and snails.
'Golden Medallion' (1984) Medium hosta with round to heart-shaped, puckered, greenish-yellow leaves and virtually white flowers. A sport of 'Tokudama Aureonebulosa'.
'Golden Scepter' (1983) Small hosta with oval to round greenish-yellow leaves and purple flowers. A good small "yellow" hosta.
'Golden Sunburst' (1984) Large hosta with heart-shaped to round, puckered, bright yellow leaves and virtually white flowers. Will not take too much sun.
'Granary Gold' (1988) Large hosta with oval to heart-shaped, greenish-yellow leaves and deep lavender flowers. Good hosta for flower arrangements.
'Green Fountain' (1979) Medium to large hosta with lance-shaped, shiny mid green leaves with tall petioles and deep lavender flowers. 'Green Fountain' is a distinctive plant.
'Green Gold' (1986) Large hosta with round to heart-shaped, puckered, green leaves edged with yellowish-cream and lavender flowers. 'Green Gold' is a sport of 'Fortunei Aureomarginata'.
'Green Sheen' (1978) Large hosta with cupped, slightly puckered leaves with a distinct waxy bloom, and pale lavender to white flowers. 'Green Sheen' more tolerant of full sun than many other "green" hostas.

'Ground Master' (1979) Medium hosta with narrow, oval leaves with wide, undulating, yellowish-cream margins that fade to white, and deep lavender-purple flowers. Highly attractive to slugs.
'Happiness' (1988) Medium hosta with heart-shaped, glaucous blue-green leaves and dark lavender flowers. Has darker flowers than most other "blue" hostas.
'Happy Hearts' (1973) Medium hosta with heart-shaped, glaucous greyish-green leaves and lavender flowers. Is good in containers.
'Hydon Sunset' (1988) Small hosta with heart-shaped, greenish-yellow leaves and dark purple flowers. Needs dappled shade.
H. hypoleuca Large Japanese species with oval or heart-shaped, pale green leaves and pale violet flowers. Can be grown in full sun.
'Invincible' (1986) Medium hosta with wedge-shaped green leaves and scented, sometimes double, lavender flowers. Resists slugs and snails.
'Iona' (1988) Large hosta with oval to heart-shaped glaucous greyish-green leaves edged with white and with lavender flowers. Good in a container.
'Kabitan' (1987) Small hosta with lance-shaped, deep-green leaves splashed with bright yellow and purple flowers. A striking plant, but needs careful cultivation.
'Lancifolia' (1888) Medium hosta with oval to lance-shaped, glossy mid-green leaves and deep violet flowers. Makes good ground cover.

'Green Sheen'

'Lemon Lime' (1988) Small or medium hosta with lance-shaped, bright greenish-yellow leaves and lavender flowers. Similar to 'Hydon Sunset' but with longer, narrower leaves.
'Little Aurora' (1978) Small hosta with heart-shaped, greenish-yellow leaves and virtually white flowers. One of the smallest "yellows".
'Marilyn' (1990) Medium to large hosta with narrowly oval to lance-shaped, yellowish-green leaves with wavy edges and pale lavender flowers. Susceptible to frost damage in cold climates.
'Masquerade' (registered 1996; formerly known as *H. venusta* 'Variegata'). Tiny hosta with lance-shaped green leaves splashed with white and lavender flowers. Tends to revert to plain green.
'Mildred Seaver' (1981) Large hosta with heart-shaped, puckered, mid-green leaves edged with creamy white; lavender flowers. A striking plant when mature.
H. montana Large Japanese species with oval, glossy dark green leaves and lavender flowers. The cultivar **'Aureomarginata'** has leaves edged with golden yellow.
'Nakaimo' (1986, but known in the West since the 1930s). Medium to large hosta with heart-shaped, mid-green leaves and pale lavender flowers. Has some of the best flowers of any hosta.
'Neat Splash' (1978) Medium hosta with oval to lance-shaped, dark green leaves edged and streaked with creamy yellow and lavender flowers. Variegation is less striking as the plant ages, so divide every three or four years.
'North Hills' (1986) Large hosta with oval to heart-shaped green leaves narrowly margined with white, and lavender flowers.
'Phyllis Campbell' (1988) Medium to large hosta with glaucous dark green leaves splashed with creamy white, and pale lavender flowers. Sometimes sold as 'Gene Summers' or 'Sharmon'.
'Pineapple Poll' (1988) Medium hosta with narrowly lance-shaped, wavy-edged, glaucous greyish-green leaves and pale lavender flowers. An unusual hosta.
H. plantaginea Large Chinese species with oval, glossy green leaves and scented white flowers. Best in full sun.
H. rectifolia Medium Japanese species with oval, glossy dark green leaves and deep violet flowers. A parent of 'Tall Boy'.
'Regal Splendor' (1987) Large hosta with broadly lance-shaped, greyish-blue leaves margined with creamy white to yellow and lilac flowers. 'Regal Splendor' is a sport of 'Krossa Regal'.
'Richland Gold' (1987) Large hosta with heart-shaped, golden yellow leaves and lavender flowers. A sport of 'Gold Standard'.
H. rohdeifolia Small Japanese species with shining dark green leaves usually edged with yellowish-cream and with lavender flowers.
'Royal Standard' (1986) Large hosta with broadly oval, glossy pale green leaves and fragrant white flowers. Grow in sun, provided the soil does

not dry out during the summer.
H. rupifraga Small Japanese species with heart-shaped dark green leaves and purple flowers. A rare, choice hosta.
'Sea Drift' (1978) Large hosta

'Shining Tot'

with oval, glossy deep green leaves with ruffled edges and lavender flowers. Good in flower arrangements.
'September Sun' (1985) Large hosta with oval to heart-shaped green leaves splashed with yellow, and pale lavender flowers. A sport of 'August Moon'.
'Serendipity' (1978) Small hosta with round to heart-shaped, glaucous blue-green leaves and deep violet flowers. One of the first hostas to emerge and to flower.
'Sherbourne Swift' (1988) Small hosta with lance-shaped, glaucous greyish-blue leaves and virtually white flowers. Makes a neat clump.
'Shining Tot' (1982) Dwarf hosta with narrowly oval, glossy dark green leaves and pale lilac flowers. Suitable for rock gardens.
'Silvery Slugproof' (1996) Medium hosta with narrowly heart-shaped, silver-blue leaves and virtually white flowers. One of the most pest-resistant hostas.
'Snow Cap' (1980) Large hosta with heart-shaped, puckered, glaucous blue-green leaves edged with creamy white, and near white flowers. Slow to establish.
'Snowden' (1988) Large hosta with heart-shaped, glaucous blue-green leaves ageing to sage green, and near white flowers. One of the grandest of all hostas.
'So Sweet' (1986) Medium hosta with oval, puckered, green leaves edged with creamy white, and fragrant white flowers. Makes a vase-shaped plant and does best in full sun.
'Spinners' (1988) Large hosta with narrowly oval leaves edged with creamy white, and lavender flowers. Is similar to 'Antioch' but more upright.
'Spritzer' (1986) Medium hosta with lance-shaped, shiny mid- to dark green leaves centrally striped with golden yellow, and pale lavender to near white flowers. An elegant hosta.
'Sugar and Cream' (1984) Large hosta with broadly oval, glossy green leaves with white margins and virtually white flowers. A sport of 'Honeybells'.
'Sultana' (1988) Small hosta with heart-shaped, mid-green leaves edged with greenish-yellow and virtually white flowers. A sport of 'Little Aurora'.
'Sweet Susan' (1986) Large hosta with heart-shaped, mid-green leaves and fragrant, purple flowers. Sometimes produces a second flush of flowers.
'Tardiflora' (1903) Small or medium hosta with narrowly lance-shaped, dark green leaves and lilac-purple flowers. Valued for its late flowering.
'Tokudama' (1940) Medium hosta with nearly round, deeply puckered, intensely glaucous blue leaves and pale lilac-grey flowers. An outstandingly beautiful hosta.
'Tokudama Aureonebulosa' (1940) Similar to 'Tokudama', but with leaves that are splashed and mottled or clouded with yellowish green.
'True Blue' (1978) Large hosta with heart-shaped, intensely glaucous blue leaves and virtually white flowers. Is similar to *H. sieboldiana* 'Elegans'.
'Undulata Albomarginata' (1987) Large hosta with oval to lance-shaped, mid-green leaves edged with creamy white and violet flowers. This hosta is sometimes known, incorrectly, as 'Thomas Hogg'.

'Snowden'

'Vera Verde' (1990) Small hosta with lance-shaped, mid-green leaves edged with creamy white, and deep lavender-purple flowers. This hosta is sometimes known, incorrectly, as *H. gracillima* 'Variegated'.
'Wogon' (1986) Small hosta with narrowly oval or lance-shaped, yellowish-green leaves and lavender flowers. A sport of *H. sieboldii*.
H. yingeri Small or medium Korean species with oval, glossy green leaves with wavy edges and lilac flowers. Tolerates sun.

Index

ACKNOWLEDGEMENTS

The publishers would like to thank Diana Grenfell for allowing photography at Apple Court Nursery, Hordle Lane, Lymington, Hants SO41 0HU (01590 642130). Apple Court Nursery, home to the National Collection of Hostas, is open to the public. Ring for opening times. Many thanks also to Ann and Roger Bowden, Cleave House, Okehampton, Devon, J.F. and L.N. Arbuthnott, Stone, Worcs; Burford House Gardens, Tenbury Wells, Worcs; Fred Ford, Ann Hartley, Mr and Mrs A. Keech of Long Buckby, Northants; Heather Montgomery, Maidwell, Northants; The Plantsman, West Haddon, Northants.